# Bygone Maidstone

Compiled from the collection of Malcolm John

John Hallewell Publications
Hallewell House
38 High Street
Chatham, Kent

ISBN 0 905540 35 2



Bygone Series (Kent)

Already available: *Bygone Medway* (Vols. one to three), *Bygone Gravesend and NW Kent*

In preparation: *Swale, Thanet, Channel Coastlands, Canterbury, Wealden District, Tunbridge Wells, Bygone Craft of Thames and Medway, Bygone Transport of Kent*

Designed and produced by Chambers Green Limited, Tunbridge Wells
Printed in Great Britain by R. J. Acford Limited, Chichester

# Introduction

Maidstone, the county town of Kent, has seen many changes since the original publication of these photographs. It is only comparatively recently that individuals and societies have become increasingly aware of the rapid erosion of individualism, of non-estate or 'plastic' developments which have changed yet hardly enhanced our town centres. Fortunately many of our villages in the central areas of Kent have escaped the perils of modernism, thus conserving our valuable rural environment.

I hope that this personal reflection, along with brief notes and jottings will bring pleasure to the residents of the Maidstone area both old and new, and foster an enthusiasm towards the environment in which they live and work.

*January 1980* *Malcolm John*

'Maidstone, in its present condition, is a pleasant, large, populous and flourishing town; it is situated in a charming vale, surrounded by distant hills; what contributes chiefly to the health and longevity of the inhabitants, is a dry soil and excellent water, free from the noxious exhalations and stagnated infection of marshy lands. It chiefly consists of four principal streets, one of which, on the gentle declivity of a hill, is remarkably neat and spacious. They are adorned with several good edifices, large inns, and the best shops in the county. The number of inhabitants in the town and parish exceeds 6,000. Linen, thread, both black and white, and tape, which is made here in great perfection, is another considerable branch of trade; besides twine, cordage, ropes and bags for hops, which are made here in great quantities.'

(1776–Seymour).

Maidstone, situated some thirty miles from London along the banks of the River Medway, is the County Town of Kent, and is the base for many Headquarters of local Kentish firms and organizations. It is primarily a market centre for agricultural goods and services from the fine agricultural land around the town. This small volume also spans the villages from Ightham and Yalding in the west to Harrietsham in the east and Cranbrook to the south.

For the sake of regularity in our volumes our pictures start on the western edge of the area, move into the town and end on the eastern side.

Let the tour commence.

Ightham is a very historic village overlooked by the primitive site of Oldbury Hill. There are many interesting houses here, including the George & Dragon Inn, Ightham Mote (possibly the perfect moated manor house), and the Old Forge, pictured above, otherwise known as 'Cookes'. This postcard shows several period carts, including one of Woodhams, the carriers with connections at Maidstone, Borough Green, Seal and Sevenoaks.

This 'posed' shot is of the Merry Boys Inn at East Peckham. Note the local brewery board 'Wateringbury Ales' and the claim for 'good beds and accommodation' with 'stall stabling'. Inside, the notice tells of a 'ploughing match'. A truly 'rural' scene, complete with window-boxes and villagers in their 'Sunday best'.

Recorded in the Domesday Book as 'Hallings', this quiet waterside village became Yaldyng in 1450. The parish lies along the banks of the River Medway. There was a William de Hampstead who owned the area of flat low ground by the stream which was valued at 1 shilling in the Lay Subsidy List of 1334.

The photographers have caught an early motor car parked in the yard of the Anchor Inn at Yalding. This rural settlement, spread over many acres, constitutes a large parish, often subjected to flooding by the Medway. The River Beult, a tributary, divides the village in two. There are several old and interesting houses in Yalding village.

The photograph shows not only the Old High Houses and the derelict corner shop prior to their demolition in 1938, but an early delivery van and shop bicycles. The fascinating history of the village is outlined in three booklets by Tony Kremer in the Twyford History Series.

Situated along the banks of the River Medway is Farleigh, lying amid the once very active 'hop-fields' of the county. Indeed, neighbouring Barming station has a house alongside the track with the 'brick-wall notice' – 'Alight here for the Hopfields of Kent'. Farleigh bridge is medieval and the fields rise steeply on each side to the church and village.

Wrotham village square nestles below the North Downs, here represented by Butts Hill. This sheltered spot was purported to be a resting place for clergy who visited the former Archbishops Palace, which was here until it was removed to Maidstone in the fourteenth century. The manor was held by the Archbishops of Canterbury until Henry VIII confiscated it later.

An unusual view taken from the church tower at Wrotham, showing the interesting architectural feature of differing roof levels – often neglected in surveys. Also apparent are the tiny windows which were a common feature up until the 1930s. With recent development of the nearby motorway, this ancient settlement will soon earn the tranquility needed for exploration.

As well as the 'march past' in West Malling High Street, it is interesting to note the traders in long aprons, the churns on the cart to the left of the picture, and how drab the buildings look in the real photograph as compared with the 'coloured view' which follows.

This view shows 'Stedmans' shop front, with gas lamps and adjacent properties with pleasing shop signs and window-boxes. Stedmans were the publishers of many postcards of the town, including our previous view. Here we have captured the elegance of old buildings, especially the Georgian influence at 'Town Malling'.

Hasted refers to Trottiscliffe (Clive) as 'a parish of no great extent containing not more than one thousand acres of land and thirty-two houses and cottages, the soil is but poor and hungry'. It is still a quiet village not far from the busy M20 motorway. This card has the name of the village spelt as it is locally pronounced – 'Trosley'.

The church and school, which so often dominate the local community, here at Birling make for a pleasant scene. The church has a perpendicular west tower which has been endowed and restored over the years by the Nevill family, who had their seat at Birling Place at the foot of the nearby Downs.

At East Malling there is a 'street called Mill Street from a corn mill there, the village has in it some tolerable good houses' – such as these in Church Walk, nestling under the guardianship of St James's Church. The house on the right has now been restored, to reveal its ancient timbering.

This card shows how popular local events were even just before the outbreak of World War I. Notice the long 'clean' dresses of the period, even being so close to the actual disaster area. Bicycles also were very popular.

Kits Coty, which stands on the slopes of Bluebell Hill between Chatham and Maidstone, has changed little over the years. Only the railings and the visitors differ from this view. It is a megalithic burial chamber, originally covered by a long barrow some 200ft long, which was still in position in the eighteenth century.

Burham's churches have a chequered history. The original parish church was alongside the river, with its few cottages and the ferries crossing the meandering river. This century saw the removal of the village to a higher level and a new church, but this too has had to close. This view is quite scarce, since it depicts the old Wesleyan Chapel.

This postcard shows what is possibly one of the most photographed sections of the River Medway. Here at Aylesford, the church stands guard over the medieval arched bridge. Sailing barges plying the river frequently berthed by the bridge below the George Inn. Just past the bridge lies The Friars where, in 1247, the European General Chapter of the Carmelites was held.

The old national school stands starkly alongside the old railway crossing on the Strood–Maidstone West line. It is rare today to see this road so empty, as Aylesford is still being strangled by the motor car and suffering from ill-sited warehouses and factory developments.

Allington Lock, near Maidstone, is a popular venue for local residents and workers alike, although the Malta Inn and the more modern lock structures now dominate the pleasing vista shown above. Nearby is the perfectly tranquil Allington Castle – retreat of the Carmelite Friars.

Always one of the important roads in Maidstone, the Tonbridge Road now has a number of educational establishments along its frontage as well as St Michael's Church built by Sir Arthur Blomfield in 1876. The trams from Maidstone to Barming once travelled along the road, and there was a depot near Barming. The trams were replaced by brown and cream trolley-buses in 1928.

St Luke's Church was built at the turn of the century, and is interesting for its wide windows and elaborate decoration. Pevsner suggests that 'the arcades would be better suited to the "music halls"' and that it has 'no delicacy of feeling'.

Sailing barges plying their trade along the Medway were once a common sight, whether their cargo was wood, coal or beer. A riverside complex of wharves and warehouses grew up to store these commodities. Sadly, much of this 'industrial' past has been lost, but we can be grateful that nearby the ancient college and church buildings survive.

The riverside at Maidstone is constantly changing to meet the needs of additional traffic. The sixties saw the clearance of Bishops Way, and Smythe and Draysons timberyard has been a car park for the market for some years. The seventies have seen a significant change, with a new bridge and improved ring road. Today's busy world allows little time to sit on the bank of the river and watch barges glide past!

This early view shows the pleasing lines of the Sessions House, now completely covered by the County Hall and offices which were erected in 1915, three years after this photograph was taken. Designed by the County Architect, F. W. Ruck, they cost some £50,000 to construct and are of ragstone faced with slabs of Portland Stone. Further inside is the County Jail.

Trinity Church, at present awaiting its fate – either to become a heritage centre or, if commercial interests remain uppermost, to be demolished and redeveloped. The church was built between 1826 and 1828, and is of semi-Italianate design, rather overshadowing the houses and hospitals which are its close neighbours.

Education has long played an important part in Maidstone's history, having been in existence since 1200. In 1348, the school building was valued at 18 shillings and four pence per annum. In 1395 the College of All Saints was founded, and in 1549 the Grammar School. The Blue Coat School followed in 1711, and since then schools and colleges have flourished. Kent Education Committee is based at Springfield, Maidstone. Can you recognise anyone in this photograph of the girls in Class I at Union Street Council Junior School?

Just above the Queen's Monument, where the traffic lights now stand on the corner of Week Street, were the original premises of Haynes & Co, now in Ashford Road. With changing fascias and street scenes, it would be interesting to see which buildings you can identify.

Horse-drawn carts had largely given way to trams in this similar view of the top of Maidstone High Street. The development of Maidstone's bus and tram system is adequately dealt with in *Tramways of Kent, Vol. 1.* The Town Hall was constructed in 1782, and the overhanging clock reminds us of the Corn Exchange in Rochester. Originally the ground floor was used as a market place.

Forming an 'E' plan, of typical Tudor proportions is Chillington Manor, an early Elizabethan house built by Nicholas Barham, and now the town's museum. There has been much restoration and many additions, although the vista is spoilt by the road and the neighbouring buildings.

On the crest of the Vale of Holmesdale rising out of the Loose Valley and Maidstone, lies Boughton Malherbe, which affords an impressive view to the South over the Weald of Kent, the 'Garden of England'.

A 'posed' group complete with roller and the usual children as 'extras' outside the nicely proportioned Unicorn Hotel. Marden stands amid fine agricultural land, and has retained its village atmosphere, probably because it is not grouped around a main road — unlike nearby Staplehurst, which has been dissected.

At one time there was a threat that a major new railway line would be placed alongside the ancient church. Happily, this was not carried out, and the churchyard area of the village retains its rural charm. Can today's children wander aimlessly in your village street?

Loose Valley has been described as the 'little Switzerland' of Kent. The original village is exceedingly pleasant, built alongside the tiny stream, with the Wool House, and the busy Chequers Inn. The church guards both these ancient houses and the more modern buildings. Read about Loose Manor in *Romance of a Tudor House* by Colonel Statham – a fascinating account.

**The College, Maidstone**

A church existed at Maidstone as early as the 11th century, and in *c.* 1208 William de Cornhill gave his mansion here as a residence for the archbishops called the Palace. Later on Archbishop Courtenay obtained a licence from Richard II to establish a college of secular canons at Maidstone, and to convert St Mary's into a collegiate church.

Malling Abbey at the eastern end of this tiny rural town is worthy of closer inspection. Malling was mentioned in the Domesday Survey when it was valued at £32 less than Maidstone and had eleven villeins and bordars working in the manor. The population of the whole area was at the time of Domesday very scanty, even Maidstone consisted of not more than a hundred houses.

TONBRIDGE ROAD MAIDSTONE, SHOWING ST MICHAEL'S CHURCH.

This fine postcard also taken along the Tonbridge Road, by St Michael's Church, shows greater detail of the corporation tramway, the brown base of the saloon of the tram-car, the curved stairway and the awesome company of passengers and two cyclists in the foreground.

**High Street — looking East**
Undoubtedly a most excellent postcard view of Maidstone, taken about 1904 looking east towards the then crossroads of the High Street and Week Street. This card also clearly shows how the town developed as an important centre of agriculture for growers and producers from the surrounding villages. The wide variety of carts and waggons can also be discerned.

Staplehurst is a linear parish, with the railway station and Victorian and later developments to the north, the church and ancient buildings to the south straddling the crest of the village, while several medieval houses nestle by the central crossroads. Staplehurst is worthy of a day's exploration, and nearby is Loddenden Manor, dating from the 16th century.

GOUDHURST FROM THE CHURCH

Goudhurst is a gem set high in the Weald. Its mature weatherboarded houses afford warmth and quietness. The large church is situated by a severe bend in the main street. This view shows the semi-square with tiled roofs and medieval chimneys. On the outskirts of the village are two 16th-century buildings, 'Pattenden' and 'Twyssenden'.

Cranbrook and its church are the 'capital and cathedral' of the Kentish Weald. There are many fine period buildings which owe their rise to the lucrative medieval wool trade. These include the Studio, an altered Wealden hall house, much weatherboarding leading around to St David Bridge, and the dominating Union Mill of 1814.

This splendid postcard view of the Old Forge at Sissinghurst depicts country life at its best. Consider the wheels and ploughshares, cart-shafts, the smell of freshly sawn timber, the cobwebs on the tiny windows, the old motorbike and the spring air wafting through the open doors from o'er the Weald.

Sissinghurst is 'Broad Highway' country. Originally named 'Saxenhurst', the famous castle was built during the reign of Henry VIII. The castle was used as a prison during the Seven Years' War, and Queen Elizabeth I visited Sissinghurst in 1573. How has the village changed? How many of the countless thousands of visitors stop to examine the village today?

Possibly one of England's finest village streets, with its buildings set back from slabs of Bethesden marble. The southern range of cottages have interconnecting attics, which enabled the ancient cloth-workers to move around freely inside the structure. The church stands at the end of this fine street, creating a complete atmosphere.

Biddenden.—Clothworkers' Hall. D B L Series 3502

Just a short distance from the main village street lies this fine range of timbered cottages dating from the early 16th century. These were combined to form the Clothworkers' Hall, whose fine tiling and overhanging gables are worthy of closer inspection. There is an exuberance of timber-framed buildings in Biddenden parish, all different and of great interest.

Another splendid street exists at Headcorn. The road from Maidstone reaches a right-angled bend at North Street, where a row of unrestored timber-framed buildings leads to the church wall and to Headcorn Manor, a fantastic Wealden house. Another fine building is Shakespeare House, shown above, with its splendid gable end.

The Church of St Peter and St Paul is a tiny building, only some 75 feet across, with the nice Filmer Chapel on the east of the south aisle. There was a Norman building here, mentioned in the Domesday Book, but little of this period remains. The prolific ecclesiastical historian, the Reverend J. Cave-Browne, the Vicar of Detling, describes the church in detail in *Sutton Valence and East Sutton,* of 1898.

The road from Maidstone to the Weald bisects the village, with the church to the west and the village to the east. There are side streets running at several levels, and the shop-front of Tantons has now been incorporated into the long fascias of 'Sutton Valence Antiques' leading up the hill towards the school.

It is interesting to compare this card with the last view, taken some two years later, and taken from further back. Sutton Valence contains the remains of a small, square Norman castle keep and some interesting Wealden houses, including the row of Lambe's almshouses dating from the end of the 16th century.

Sutton Valence school was founded in 1578 by William Lambe, a clothworker from London. The school now occupies a site at the northern entrance to the village, and the site was operative from 1914.

Sutton Valence Mill was rebuilt in 1798; the original probably dated from *c* 1720. There was a strange event reported in the *Kent Messenger* – 'a lady artist, seated on the gallery surrounding it, sketching the Weald to the south, then someone without knowing started the mill, and the enormous sweep killed her instantly'.

Several old cottages still cluster around the wide village green. Some are half-timbered, whilst others show Georgian elegance. The history of this interesting village appeared recently in *Bearsted and Thurnham* published by the local history society.

The remains of Boxley Abbey walls cover a wide area, the building being noted for two 'wonder-working images', the Rood of Boxley and a figure of St Romwold. The great barn may have been the guesting house in monastic days. The remains, recently excavated, were the only Cistercian Abbey buildings in Kent (from *Around Historic Kent*).

Thurnham is a small hamlet close by the Pilgrim's Way, with an ancient earthwork known as Thurnham Castle. There are some more remains about a mile away at Binbury. Here at the foot of the North Downs, there are open views southwards towards the Weald, these are traversed by narrow roads such as Ware Street, depicted above in 1909.

Harrietsham is a village alongside the main road from Maidstone which once had a wealth of period houses. Some of them remain, but even in the early years of this century some were being dismantled. The building on the extreme left is a fine example of a Hall house, with sloping beams and tiled roof.

Productivity was measured by the necessity to eat and survive. Often colourful characters 'imported' from London and other cities joined the local farmers, labourers and children to work the fields. Many stayed in huts or slept in the open for the whole season, others came by train and were shipped to the station in waggons.

Sunday was their day of rest, and even those who were reluctant to make the effort to attend church were not overlooked, as wandering pastors ministered to their wayward flock 'on site'. Farleigh Bridge witnessed them washing clothes, children, pots and pans and hanging their faded garments on bushes along the water's edge. Can this really be replaced by machines?

**Leeds Castle**

This fairyland castle set in the very heart of the Kentish countryside has a long and interesting history described in our "Castles in Kent". During the civil war the Castle was the residence of Sir John Culpeper who was a Royalist but it was used by the Parliament as a prison. This century has seen the Castle used as an international conference centre providing strict security.

## THE HISTORY OF MAIDSTONE

Being a limited reprint of 1,000 copies of the 1881 original work by Russell, the book has since been reprinted as a second limited edition. Maidstone is the county town of Kent, playing an important part in the history of Kent, yet not receiving the attention of writers and historians to any great degree. Newton's and then Russell's books have become avidly sought after in the antiquarian field, and it is hoped that this volume will meet the need in providing the basic background to the town's history. It is a companion volume to our reprinted histories of Rochester and Strood. It is hard-backed and contains some 420 pages with several line drawings. It costs £10.00 from the publishers, John Hallewell Publications at 38 High Street, Chatham, Kent (add 60p postage and packing), or from your local bookshop.

If you have enjoyed this book, may we introduce you to

## AROUND HISTORIC KENT

compiled by Malcolm John and illustrated by Rochester artist C. A. T. Brigden. This traveller's guide and introduction to the country forms part of the 'Around Historic . . . ' popular series of books. There are over 120 descriptions, each with its own special drawing. The author takes particular care to ensure that the important lesser-known features of places are mentioned, and the book represents miles of enjoyable countryside which have been travelled to ensure authenticity.

The author and illustrator have just completed their second 'Around Historic . . . ' book, this time describing the interesting people, places and buildings of the Thames Valley.

The book is hardbacked and contains 136 pages. It can be obtained price £3.95 from the publishers at 38 High Street, Chatham, Kent (add 50p postage and packing), or from your local bookseller.